the Register and the Ledger: Single Entry Accounting for Home and Business Economics

2nd Edition

Taught at Western Colorado Community College
2019 and 2020
By Aaron Scott Brachfeld Michelson

<u>for Frieda Nora</u>
flint's firelight is struck by iron
by fire iron steels
as I hope you shall.
my iron Lady, iron rusts
by tears and sweat and blood
this is why you must steel yourself
so strike now - and hard - and have no doubt
you shall inspire your own illumination

ISBN: 9781708166977

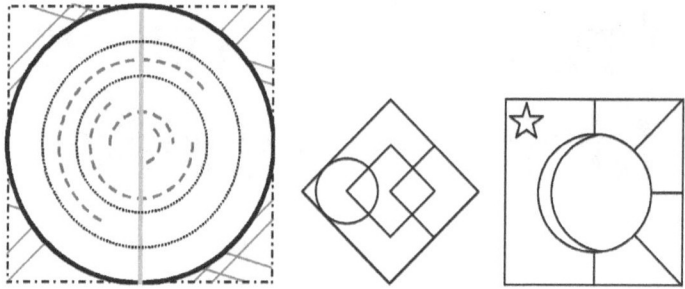

Published by Loka Hatha Yoga in Grand Junction, Colorado

There are many suitable places for your meditation.
We hope this becomes one of them.
Anguttara Nikaya 1.159

LOKAHATHAYOGA@GMAIL.COM
lokahathayoga.blogspot.com

© 2019, 2020 by Aaron Scott Brachfeld Michelson

ownership retained by author, rights granted for unlimited publication, use and sale to Loka Hatha Yoga to further its non-profit purposes.

TABLE OF CONTENTS

Chapter 1: the Purpose of the Ledger   5
   CHAPTER SUMMARY   5
   A brief introduction to
   the theory of accounting   6
   The development of information   16
      What is information?   17
   Useful information:
   the objects of analysis   18
   Monetary and non-monetary activity   19
   Types of Ledgers   19

Chapter 2: the Register   21
   CHAPTER SUMMARY   21
   Don't Skip This Chapter: Philosophy of Mathematics   22
   Basic and Advanced Addition   22
      Addition, subtraction, and division   22
      Theory of conversion: comparing apples to oranges   23
      Multiplication and division   24
      Special circumstances: Multiplication by zero   25
      Special circumstances: Multiplication by one   25
      Special circumstances: Negative Addition   26
      Special circumstances: Division by zero   26
      Special circumstances: Division by one   26
      Special circumstances: Negative Quantities   27
      Philosophical implications of zero   28

Chapter 3: Computation   **29**
   CHAPTER SUMMARY   29
   The methodology of computation   30

Registering using paper and pencil	31
Registering using digital spreadsheets	33

Chapter 4: Reducing Expenses and Waste with Registers 38

CHAPTER SUMMARY 38

Skills of data categorization and application to taxes and food waste 39

> What is a category of data? What is the accuracy of data? Examples of income, expense, dates, non-quantitative data 39
>
> Methodology of categorization 41

Reducing expenses using ledgers 42

Principles of preparing a report 45

> To be held accountable 45
>
> Empower others to understand sufficiently for analysis, decision making and action within their role 46
>
> Consider the person's role:
> to whom and for what are they accountable? 47

Color coding 49

Chapter 5: Improving Efficiency with Registers 50

CHAPTER SUMMARY 50

Management theory 51

Method of analysis: the regression 52

> Analysis of regressive equation:
> understanding relative importance 52

Capitalism 54

Dependent Variable 55

Independent Variable 55

Analysis 56

> Analysis of regressive equation: understanding trends 56

Surplus resources	57
Calculating if a resource is surplus	57
Introduction to finance	58
Having resources when they are required: preventing interruption	59
Using ledger for financial analysis	60
Chapter 6: Resource Theory	**61**
CHAPTER SUMMARY	61
Introduction to economics	62
Recognizing renewable and non-renewable resources	64
Theory of exhaustion	64
Calculating point of exhaustion: the intersection with zero	66
Regressive analysis on increasing inefficiency	67
The emergency expense (unanticipated zeroing of resource)	67
Theory: reduce use of non-renewable resources, rely on renewable resources	68
Conclusion: Capitalism	**69**

Chapter 1: the Purpose of the Ledger

CHAPTER SUMMARY

A brief introduction to the history of accounting, and the development of information economics. Accounting's modern purpose is to provide the accountant with useful information of both monetary and non-monetary activity for analysis. The object of this analysis is the reduction of both the rate and quantity of money and resources which are spent or wasted, and the simultaneous increase of both the rate and quantity of money and resources which are acquired. Accounting's secondary purpose is to assist in taxation preparation, and the communication of financial information with others involved in decision making.

Whether at home or in business, if you reduce your expenses and increase your available resources, you'll become wealthy. This requires nothing more than addition and subtraction using a ledger, and the other easy-to-understand state-of-the-art economic principles in this book. Whether you prefer paper and pencil or Google Sheets on the cloud, you should learn how to use these tools better to better yourself.

This book will provide an introduction to the theory, system and techniques of the ledger: understand, then, that the money you have is only worth what it can buy, and if that which is bought cannot be enjoyed, the money is worthless. Therefore, it is the information which can be learned from the ledger, rather than the balance of it, which matters most. Consequently, this book will focus on the **single entry ledger, and the process of capitalization**, that the systems of capitalism might be instructed: it is the act of **transforming assets and liabilities into wealth worth having** which should be the object of your effort.

A brief introduction to the theory of accounting

The first step in accounting is **taking inventory** of what you have: this is your starting capital. And even if you have nothing of value, you will account for your capacity for work, your labor, your own self.

For, you see, the science of economics grew out of the end of Feudalism, at the dawn of the scientific revolution when all across the world peasants freed themselves from their Masters. Therefore it should be unsurprising that the most basic premise of the science of economics is that all people are by nature free men and women, and when permitted to enjoy this state of liberty, owning themselves, every person has the motivation and capacity to self-improve and obtain what they require - by industry or trade - and should hold themselves and those they work and trade with accountable to their obligations.

This process of accounting was much older: it is the fourth oldest profession in the world. People first learned to produce things of value, then trade for them in commerce, then perform services for those undertaking commerce. At this point, people needed to trust someone to perform the service, even if it was themselves, of accounting for such income and expenses as had become commonplace in business.

A contract for an installment payment plan in the purchase of 3131 bushels of barley over 37 months. The duration of the loan is separated from the other terms by a box, similar to how we would separate using lines or spreadsheet cells for clarity. The officiating seal being affixed over the text remains a custom today by notaries, as does the standard contents of the receipt. Very little has changed in business principles since the stone age, though sophistication, art and skill has improved.

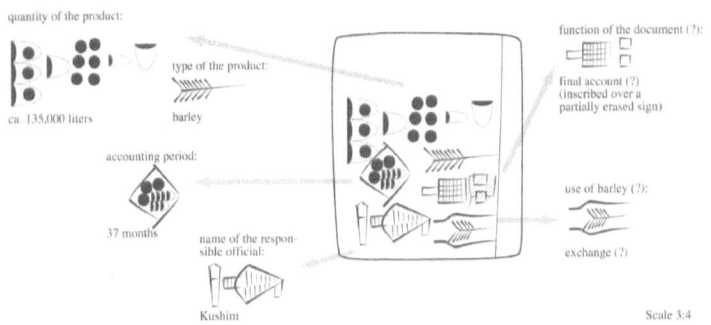

quantity of the product:
ca. 135,000 liters
type of the product:
barley
accounting period:
37 months
name of the responsible official:
Kushim

function of the document (?):
final account (?) (inscribed over a partially erased sign)
use of barley (?):
exchange (?)

Scale 3:4

Long before money was invented, long before numbers were invented, valuables were stored in jars or buildings, and crude markings were used to first count, then track the quantity inside. These crude markings were also used in the practices of commerce and service. Such tracking and counting provided security against theft, provided a trusted third-party witness of delivery in a primitive form of invoicing, and helped inform the owner on the decisions required for their businesses.

This is because when the quantity of a valuable was known, it could be easily determined if it were taken illegally or contrary to agreement, and when, and therefore by whom. And this helped keep people accountable to their actions. And if the owner understood how much inventory he had, or raw materials, they could anticipate how to use this surplus needs or plan around their deficiencies - and both earn more profit and keep their contractual agreements.

This trust was essential as society organized: written records which could not be easily tampered with allowed supervisors and employers to trust their employees and business partners to trust each other. Contracts which were witnessed by the government permitted even greater trust - and penalties for breach.

Eventually, the system was expanded to track valuables which were not easily put into jars or buildings, like livestock, or crops growing in a field. Warehousing was begun, where a person could own something in a building or field owned by someone else. These third parties began to facilitate trade of ownership without the actual movement of these valuables: a person could simply write on a tablet or piece of paper that they sold ownership of those items to someone else, and received something of value for that sale, and that was that.

This is how money was invented: coins, usually of metal, were easily transferred and traded even when the valuables they were buying were not.

Metals were usually used because they could be divided into microscopic parts, and recombined by melting - without losing value. Their purity was easily discovered using simple chemistry. Though, in many places, gemstones and precious rocks like jade were and continue to be used, the world over Group 11 metals (gold, silver and copper) were and remain the primary currency because of these unique properties.

And this is how a philosophy grew around the practice of business, wherein people became accountable to their actions: through karma, sin, and other senses of duty, and the idea of the truthfulness, the honor, the shine, of a metal could be trusted as well. Many religious and cultural concepts grew out of this system of accounting.

With the innovation of numbers, and later mathematics, quantities of valuables could be tracked or even anticipated and an increasingly scientific understanding of time allowed for the innovation of finance, and a more sophisticated understanding of the world developed.

When taxation was invented, the government began to look upon false records as a crime, even dishonesty as a crime. Therefore, a system of forensic accounting was developed to understand whether taxpayers were being honest and to hold them accountable in their accounting. Gradually, the practices of accounting were gradually standardized for the convenience of the government tax collectors - so they didn't have to learn how each business owner was keeping records. Forms were made, and the first laws codified.

As world trade developed in the bronze age after the invention of the "corporation," and both governments and these new business entities undertook international commerce with each other globally, local standard methods of accounting were gradually standardized into an international form, and eventually people all around the world began to use the same numbers for business - even if at home they spoke different languages. This universal language facilitated the transfer of numerical information by use of "invoices," "bills," "books" and other documentation.

This permitted the understanding that the owners of a business held a stake or share in the capital of that business: It was discovered **Capital = Assets − Liabilities**. Journals were made to document activities that affected assets or liabilities and measure capital - the single entry ledger.

However, it would not be until the year 1340 in Genoa that the growing use of finance and leveraging eliminated most capital from the equation: in the economy, debts now exceeded assets. The economy was one which functioned through lending: we evolved beyond the use of currency and into the financial age. This modern age required a modern system of measuring capital be invented: the double entry ledger.

Though it should be admitted that the Genoan method has its roots in a Florentine method developed by Giovanno Farolfi & Company, a Merchant Bank, for their office in Nimes, the Genoan method "completed" the process of compiling the ledger into useful reports.

In double entry ledgers, every action is measured twice: how they affect capital becomes secondary. The accountant's primary responsibility is to provide information on how an action affects assets and liabilities: it is assumed and understood that these will balance, or equal. Granted, excess is still understood as Capital, but what is important here is that the mindset had shifted to one of a financial economy.

Today, arabic numbers are typically used around the world no matter whether the person speaks arabic at home, and a system of accounting developed on the Italian peninsula is generally preferred even if the nation has no allegiance to any Italian government. This system of accounting is based upon the single entry ledger.

As the new financial economy, a new "fiat" currency emerged, surpassing Group 11 metals. Now, though gold, silver and copper were still used, and accepted, to transact financial business you did not need to exchange coins. And because everyone was now participating in the financial economy, you did not even need gold, silver or copper to buy and sell things, only notes with the bank to whom you and your fellow merchant owed those coins to - just like before, with the warehouse, cattle and grain did not need to change hands, coins now were warehoused in banks.

Bankers discovered quickly they could trust their members who had borrowed their funds to pay the borrowed sums back with interest: with this trust, the bankers felt confidence to lend money they were not in possession of, but would be in the future. Now, where there was one coin lent out at interest, there were in fact two in circulation: one which would be paid back to the bank, and the other in circulation lent out in trust. This doubling of the monetary supply made things cheaper to buy, and fueled economic growth: both creditor and debtor could use the same coin at the same time. So long as both could be confident in the honor of their business partners.

Some banks, in confidence, lent their money not once, not twice, but even dozens of times. Or hundreds. Banks still do this today. And some puissant banks will even lend and borrow against money that is lent to another - through derivatives. Or by selling bonds against the future earnings of interest. Such revenue streams we enjoy today would have been quite beyond the imaginations of our ancestors, though the principles are identical: consider, then, what new revenues await those bold enough to seek them?

This confidence was rewarded with success. So bankers were encouraged to experimentation and exploration: by the most rudimentary economic methodology, they discovered they could trade interests in commodities in the future: it was possible to pre-sell and pre-buy crops, cattle, ore and other materials. This led to futures markets, and market stabilization and reduced risks for producers - which permitted further economic expansion. And when these futures were permitted to be traded as derivatives or borrowed against at interest, it effectively increased the supply of money further, fueling further growth. Now, where there was one coin, hundreds or thousands were in circulation.

Success encourages confidence, and soon not only commodities and coins were traded and lent, but interests in commercial and industrial enterprises through preferred stock and corporate bonds - these also increased the of money, and fueled even more growth. This encouraged corporate banking to develop - and flourish. Innovations in insurance permitted by corporate banking reduced risks even further, stimulating even greater confidence, and innovation - leading to an incredible rate of economic expansion: where one coin existed, millions were in circulation.

In those magnificent days of discovery of the early financial economy, there seemed to be no limit to economic expansion. But eventually, by the first century B.C., these banks began to amass more capital than their local governments and were seen as threats. Or at least rivals.

In the power struggle that followed, banks were gradually brought under the control of governments, who issued their own fiat currencies. The first government to do this was in what is today China. In 210 BC, Emperor Qin Shi Huang abolished all forms of currency except his own coins, which he decided would have a particular value regardless of their metalic worth. Other governments around the world, from Europe and Africa to Oceana, saw this success and emulated it. Globally, financial markets began to be regulated, and so did the corporations that issued stock and bonds.

Twelve centuries later, in 1024, paper money that had been developed by bankers in China (they called it "flying money" - it tended to blow away) also began to be controlled by the government. By the Yuan Dynasty, in 1260 AD, the government abolished all forms of money except their own printed Chao, the first fiat paper currency.

With paper money, each sheet of paper could represent a microscopic amount of gold, silver or copper - or even divide gemstones into unitary quantities. Now, the value of the gold, silver, copper and gems which had been the foundation of worth were now so far divided through trade that the monetary units they represented had no real value: units of currency were worth far less than could physically be measured. So a new understanding of value had to be developed.

Do fiat currencies have real value? Certainly. You can buy things with them - and in fact, you have to. Because if you don't, you lose things of real value, like your freedom. Trust, credit, is earned - or commanded. And to the extent that the government can enforce its currency laws, the currency has trust, or credit.

Enforcing this trust became of national interest. And so by July 1854, with the innovation of the limited liability company, the role of accountants could include many paralegal and legal responsibilities: the modern Certified Public Accountant was born when The Institute of Accountants in Glasgow was formed. It was formed to provide assurance that their professional associates were competent to their new responsibilities.

By 1880, the Institute of Chartered Accountants in England and Wales was formed for similar purpose. 7 years later, a similar association was formed in America.

Today, the profession is highly regulated, requiring government license, and the numerous associations today work together to ensure greater homogeneity and consistency in our ever-increasingly global economy.

Today we are on the verge of a new currency: as information itself becomes valuable, we may expect innovations to quantify the value of data. This revolution may come tomorrow, or in hundreds of years - but is inevitable. For as we discover things of value, or that things lack value, our understanding of how to measure these values must evolve. And with this evolution, we will discover new wealth, and our economy will again expand. The universe is infinite, and so is our capacity to see what is good and valuable in it.

However, the basic principles of accounting for that value will forever remain a touchstone of our ancient past: though we use paper and computers today, and our ancestors used actual stones, we will still use the same ledger system they did. And, conceivably, our distant descendants always will.

The development of information

A ledger is a word that means "to lay," in how a holy book is left laying about in a church for the laity to read, or financial documents at a corporation are left laying about for anyone to read. The reason we read these books is because we desire information.

Before the ledger, records were sealed, sometimes physically in clay or wax balls or jars. This was to prevent tampering: tokens or records were placed in, and retrieved during audits. Of course, fraud was still possible. And later, with paper, fraud was still possible, even with ink, and sewing individual records together into "books" or "sutras." With each innovation of record keeping, fraud becomes more difficult. But it has been found transparency and multiple records makes fraud impossible - which is why the innovation of "block chain" and other digital innovations revolutionized the reliability of records.

In the long history of accounting, the most valuable service provided by an accountant or bookkeeper is the development of information from the raw financial data in a home or business.

Financial record keepers are not only servants, but producers: they produce information from data. The quality and usefulness of this product of information is one of the primary considerations of their profession.

What is information?

Information is different than data in that it formulates data through a process of calculation to reveal relationships between data. These relationships represent new data which had not been directly observed: this new data produced is "information."

So, we may have the data that $A = B$, and the other data that $B = C$, and from this we may produce the information that $A = C$. And from this we may produce additional information that $C+B = 2A$. And eventually even produce information that because $2A = D$, $D+C+B = 4A$. And so forth.

Because the relationship between data can be used to affect the expenses or income, the value of this information is sometimes greater than the effort used to produce it.

In other words, a business owner will pay to obtain information which could earn them more money by efficiently reducing costs or by generating more income through affecting one variable in their production, trade or service - or put in the time to learn how to produce such information themselves (as you are doing).

But sometimes information is not worth the expense of its development. Therefore, information must be obtained efficiently and in a cost-effective and easy way - and be very useful.

The data which is used for developing information is categorized through a "ledger." The ledger eases the process by which relationships between income, expense and the many things that can affect those, including time, may be calculated.

Useful information: the objects of analysis

Not all information is equally useful. In developing data into information, try to remember the purpose for your effort. Some common purposes include:

- Reducing of both the rate and quantity of money and resources spent or wasted
- Increasing both the rate and quantity of money and resources which are acquired
- Taxation preparation
- Communicating financial information with others involved in decision making.

One category of data which will almost always be useful for information is the date or time of activity: understanding relationships and trends through time can reveal the factors involved. Other categories which are useful are the quantity of valuables which are expended or are earned, and those particular activities or people or machines which earn or expend valuables - this permits comparison between methods of income and expense.

From this we should understand that the role of the bookkeeper or accountant is not only to accurately collect data, but to anticipate the needs of those who would require its information.

Monetary and non-monetary activity

Valuables subject to the activity registered in the ledger are either monetary or non-monetary. Non-monetary valuables can be converted into their monetary values: for example, the value of a slice of bread might be understood to be the percent of the loaf it represents multiplied by the cost of the loaf. A bushel of wheat might be understood in terms of the average price a buyer might pay for it today. In converting non-monetary and monetary values, remember that the value of money, the amount of goods it will buy, does change through time. And that these are not fixed ratios, even at one particular time: for example, a loaf of bread is not the same price at all stores, even if that loaf of bread is the same type and brand.

Here, it is only important to understand that the numerical values in a ledger may be used to describe either money or non-money items.

When non-monetary or monetary items are categorized with the additional data of a date or other measure of time, activity is observed: using a ledger, one may understand how the quantities change over time, and other activity of these items. The act of recording these changes is frequently described as "registering" them. This is basically an act of journaling observations.

Types of Ledgers

There are five principle types of ledgers: those which account for assets, liabilities, income, expenses, and capital.

For example, an income type ledger might record sales in a sales ledger, or accounts receivable in an accounts receivable ledger. Or an expense ledger might record purchases in a purchase ledger.

These ledgers are combined into a "General Ledger" which aids in the calculation of capital.

The report of these is undertaken through a process called "auditing," from the word used to describe the oral presentations given by ancient accountants (audire = to hear).

In a financial economy, these reports are made for two purposes: for those who owe money (debtors), and those who trust others to pay them back (creditors).

The debtor has need for different information than the creditor. We will focus on the needs of debtors: households and small businesses.

Chapter 2: the Register

CHAPTER SUMMARY

An introduction to the mathematics required for the registering of both monetary and non-monetary transactions. Specifically, addition and subtraction.

Don't Skip This Chapter: Philosophy of Mathematics

It is tempting to skip a chapter containing basic skills, but this chapter will instruct in the **philosophy of mathematics**, that is, the **science of logic** which is so necessary to good accounting.

Basic and Advanced Addition

Addition, subtraction, and division

Addition is the process by which items are quantified and then combined. It is this process of quantification and combination which is the foundation of accounting - and therefore the methodology used in quantification and combination is very important.

For example, a person may possess basket of oranges and a basket of apples. Quantifying these by accounting for them, by counting them, the person will understand they have 10 apples and 15 oranges. Combining these through addition, they may accurately say they have a sum of 25 fruits.

Similarly, when items are quantified and individualized or separated, we undertake a process of subtraction or division.

If we have 10 apples, but half of them are of a superior grade, and the other of an inferior grade, we may subtract the inferior apples from the superior apples, and re-quantify the superior apples in a process of division to understand we have 5 superior apples, or half our apples are superior. Similarly, we may remove from our 10 apples those unsuited for sale, and requantify to understand we may sell only 5 of our 10 apples.

Theory of conversion: comparing apples to oranges

As just observed, all quantities can be numerically combined, whether it is money and non-money items, or apples and oranges. It is true that any thing may be converted into numerical values. And also into monetary values. And these two, money and numbers, are different.

If the value of apples is $1 per fruit and oranges are valued at $2 per fruit, the person may convert their sum of 25 fruits to say they have $40 - in fruit. Until they realize this value by actually selling or buying these fruits, they remain unconverted, but may still be considered in terms of their monetary worth. It is theoretically possible to convert any thing of value into its monetary equivalent.

Land may be estimated to be worth so many dollars based upon its usefulness, or ability to yield monetary value. Even a human life may be so quantified - in terms of earning power or by any other means of assessing its value to a consumer, provider, buyer or seller. And these lives frequently are, when a person decides to purchase life insurance - or pays the penalty of manslaughter in the courts.

However, just as we may accurately say that one life is worth more money than another, or an apple is worth more or less money than an orange, or that these values are greater or less in one market than another, it is nevertheless true that money is not the only means of assessing value.

Therefore, while it is true that any item may be converted to its monetary value, assessing its value beyond the terms of money is frequently necessary to decision making. Nevertheless, these non-monetary valuations may be just as easily quantified: we may say, with confidence, that one life is not worth more or less than another - that all people are equal.

Understanding the unrealized value of a thing is accomplished by assessing its worth - a process which has not yet been fully or scientifically standardized, but which future accountants may yet discover.

Multiplication and division

Multiplication is the process by which we add the addition of added sums: it is a process of repeatedly combining quantified values. If we add one apple to another, we possess the sum of 2 fruits. If we have a sum of 2 fruits, and add it to an equal sum, we possess 4 fruits. We may say that we added the addition of 2 apples to our sum of 2 apples.

In saying it this way, we clearly expose our process and method, we show the quantities and combinations as they were made. $2 \times 2 = 4$ is much different than simply saying 4, or even saying $2 + 2 = 4$. Because in the former, we may clearly see we are saying 2 identical groups of apples x 2 = 4 apples, whereas in the latter it becomes difficult to know whether we are adding 2 different types of apples, or even two different types of fruits.

This making things into units is the foundational concept to multiplication.

In multiplication, we employ the method of units: it is easier to call 125 apples a bushel, and it is easier math to combine two bushels to possess 250 apples than it is to add 2+2 for 125 times. We therefore say, 1 bushel 2 times because it is easier to understand.

The reverse may be done in a process of division, where subtraction is undertaken in series: we know that 250 apples results in 2 groups of 125 apples when we divide the 250 apples into groups of 125 apples - and discover it can be done twice.

Presenting information in the simplest, but also the most effective, terms is essential for good communication.

Special circumstances: Multiplication by zero

The discovery of zero radically altered the methods of multiplication and addition. Now, the lack of something was itself something: instead of observing that we lacked apples, we observed that we had no or zero apples. To have 1 bushel zero times is to have zero bushels at all. Any multiplication of zero results in zero. Zero bushels is the same as zero apples, which is the same as zero truck loads of apples, which is the same as zero boatloads of apples.

This is why to have no thing is different than to lack something: when we lack an apple, it may mean we are one apple shy of a bushel. Or one apple shy of a boatload. This is not the same as having no apples at all. But it is to say we do not have a boatload.

Properly converting numbers into information requires discerning the difference between something and nothing.

Special circumstances: Multiplication by one

Similarly, to have a single unit of something is to possess the full unit of that thing: to say we have a bushel of apples does not mean we have a bushel and one apple. In developing information, precision is important: we must understand what it is that is being observed. At least to a reasonable degree: depending on the circumstances, it may be allowable to call 124 apples a full 1 bushel. Or even to call 100 apples a full 1 bushel. Understanding these circumstances is as large a part of the accountant's work as the process of summation.

Special circumstances: Negative Addition

This is why we may undertake negative addition. When we owe a quantity of apples, we own fewer apples than we possess. So, you can possess one apple, but owing one apple, own zero apples: $1 + -1 = 0$. This is much different than saying we possess no apples: for, in fact, we are in possession of many apples, but owe them all. In developing information, the method by which a quantity is obtained matters as much or more than the quantity itself.

Special circumstances: Division by zero

Dividing by zero is technically infeasible, but is undertaken with the understanding that we are simply undertaking no division, rather than dividing a quantity of items into zero units.

Special circumstances: Division by one

Similarly, we may always divide a group of things into one combined unit: if we have 30 apples, and call 30 apples a "box," we then have 1 box of apples.

If we call 7.5 hours a workday, we can erroneously estimate that we work the same number of workdays as someone who calls 8 hours a workday. This is sometimes a successful method of fraud, and frequently an honest error: in any case, division by 1 should be avoided.

This combination into units is the principle purpose and achievement of division - but it is not usually useful to reduce everything into one single unit.

Special circumstances: Negative Quantities

When we owe someone something we do not have, it is lent to us on trust - in "credit."

To possess such a negative quantity of something requires special rules for addition, subtraction, multiplication and division.

Multiplying any positive unit by any negative unit will result in a negative quantity; when we are in debt, we only speak of things in terms of our debt. If we owe 2 apples, any quantity of these units would result in us owing more apples: to owe 4 units of 2 apples would mean to owe 8 apples. In this way, too, division of a positive quantity with a negative quantity will result in a negative quantity.

However, a negative multiplied by a negative or divided by a negative will result in a positive quantity: when we owe 2 apples, and have given up 4 units of 2 apples, we actually possess 8 apples (yes, it includes the 2 apples we owe: we cannot give up what we do not have in our possession - as previously discussed, to owe 2 apples and possess 2 apples are different things).

Adding a negative quantity to a positive quantity reduces that positive quantity; subtracting a negative quantity from a positive quantity increases that positive quantity. When we no longer owe an apple, we are one apple wealthier.

Philosophical implications of zero

The illogicalities which reveal themselves through in mathematical calculation have resulted in profound philosophical understandings.

The concept that "all is one" developed when the understanding of zero was theoretical: dividing all the integers, positive and negative, from the smallest quantity to the largest, when zero is not included, results in the number -1. The reason given that zero is theoretical is that it cannot be proven: you cannot divide a quantity by nothing, or into nothing.

Similarly, all is nothing developed with the understanding that zero is a real number: multiplying all integers, including zero, results in the number zero. The reason given that zero is real is that it can be proven: you can have no units of something, or have nothing of something.

This paradox of zero, that it can both be proven and not be proven, resulted in a profound understanding of simultaneity, relativity, relevance, and a modern perspective of interdependence. Even though integers were infinite in both positive and negative, the balance of positive and negative could be assumed, and this implied a connection or interdependence between all things.

Modern mathematics has developed this and other feats of logic into game theory to develop a sophisticated modern ethical philosophy, founded in economics.

Chapter 3: Computation

CHAPTER SUMMARY

Understanding the methodology of computation required for registering, whether for digital spreadsheets like Google Sheets and Excel, or on paper.

The methodology of computation

Computation is a method by which multiple calculations are performed: this methodology, or computation, is undertaken by algorithms, or a process or set of rules. The process by which a method is accomplished matters more than the method itself - just as the method matters more than the result, for the method affects the result, and the process affects the method.

In example, 2 + 3 / 4 x 5 - 6 could equal any number of things if we did not say what action, multiplication, division or subtraction is undertaken first.

Put another way, calculation is the determination or assessment of a quantity. Computation is the manner in which calculation is undertaken.

The method of calculation is well understood, and with the wide availability of simple electronic calculators, largely unnecessary to understand at a theoretical level. However, the method of computation is important for an accountant to understand.

The method typically used for computation by an accountant is called "registering," a word which implies the understanding that economic phenomena are being observed and journaled. Due to the nature of economic phenomena, some of these phenomena have not yet occurred: we are able to anticipate future production, future trades and even borrow this future wealth for present use - or apply it in arrears to the past. It is theoretically possible to anticipate the entire history of humanity's economic activity - to some greater or lesser degree of accuracy, as the science of economics advances.

But this is the reason why journaling is the foundational method of computation: it is the time at which things have, are, or will occur that matters most.

Registering using paper and pencil

Though specialized lined paper is available for registering with paper and pencil, these conveniences hinder the learning process.

First, consider the data you would collect in your journal. The most important data is the date that an observation corresponds to. These will be collected in a column. On your paper, create a column heading, and label it "DATE"

DATE

The next data you would collect would likely involve the income or expense of funds or things of value. These should also have columns.

DATE   **INCOME**   **EXPENSE**

Finally, you would likely benefit from notation or other soft data describing what was observed: for example, answering the questions, who, what, where, how and why there was income or expense. When is already answered in the date: similarly, each of these notes can be broken out into separate categories of data.

Soft data can be analyzed later to produce information: the easiest way to do this is to combine soft data into categories: such as by combining transactions by financial quarter, grouping transactions with individual suppliers or creditors you frequently undertake business with, or organizing the data by materials frequently traded, by places business is undertaken, etc. etc.: Provide a column for this data soft data as well.

DATE   NOTE   INCOME   EXPENSE

I included it next to the date to ease communication: in reading the data, the reader will first understand when something occurred, then get a note to understand what happened, and see the income or expense which was observed.

Now, the data is being collected in rows. It would ease informational production to correlate each information with each data.

The first information which might be collected is a running balance of funds: how much wealth do you have at the end of each transaction of income or expense? This can be added anywhere, but would likely facilitate communication best by being added near to the income and expense.

DATE   NOTE   INCOME   EXPENSE   BALANCE

The balance information is computed by a process of calculation

BALANCE = PREVIOUS BALANCE + INCOME - EXPENSE

This formula requires taking an initial inventory of wealth to obtain an initial balance.

Here is an example, showing the calculations:

DATE	NOTE	INCOME	EXPENSE	BALANCE
Jan 1	Inventory			$500
Jan 1	Grocery		$100	=$500-$100=$400
Jan 2	Salary	$200		=$400+$200=$600
Jan 3	Insurance		$20	=$600-$20=$580

But it is not necessary to always show your work:

DATE	NOTE	INCOME	EXPENSE	BALANCE
Jan 1	Inventory			$500
Jan 1	Grocery		$100	$400
Jan 2	Salary	$200		$600
Jan 3	Insurance		$20	$580

We can then produce information in numerous ways: the total income can be developed by summing the income column (it is $200), the total expenses can be developed by summing the expenses column ($120), and this can prove the balance of $580 when it is seen that $500 + $200 - $120 = $580. There is a lot of useful information which can be developed with this little bit of data, but that will be addressed in its proper place.

Registering using digital spreadsheets

Digital spreadsheets are a convenience to the modern accountant that the ancients could not have even dreamed of. A computing machine simultaneously accepts and undertakes complex calculations, almost instantaneously, presenting data and aiding in informational production through analysis!

Two of the most common spreadsheet programs in use are Excel (made by Microsoft Corporation) and Googlesheets (made by the Alphabet Corporation). Because Googlesheets is free, and provides sufficient and similar service for the basic needs of a register, it is easy to endorse the latter over the former. This said, Excel is a superior product - and, depending on the complexity of your needs, may be the necessary choice. However, they all function using the same basic principles, and the lessons here are designed to be applicable to all major spreadsheet programs.

The only difference between using a spreadsheet and paper is that data is input by typing, and calculations are input as formulations, sometimes using references to other cells - which requires understanding their row number and column letter.

Since there are many excellent classes and books on how to use these programs efficiently, the scope here will be limited to how to apply these programs in making and keeping a ledger.

	A	B	C	D	E
1	DATE	NOTE	INCOME	EXPENSE	BALANCE
2	1/1	Inventory			$500
3	1/1	Grocery		$100	$400
4	1/2	Salary	$200		$600
5	1/3	Insurance		$20	$580

You can see by the example above that it greatly resembles the written form - except that each line is numbered by a "row" number, and each column is lettered by a "column" letter. These combine to make coordinates, which can be referenced in formulas: to reference the $100 grocery expense, we may describe the cell D3.

If you look closely at the data in the balance column, you will see it is in fact a formula for computation which uses these very references.

	A	B	C	D	E
1	DATE	NOTE	INCOME	EXPENSE	BALANCE
2	1/1	Inventory			$500
3	1/1	Grocery		$100	=E2+C3+D3
4	1/2	Salary	$200		=E3+C4+D4
5	1/3	Insurance		$20	=E4+C5+D5

The student of pen and paper, or even pencil and paper, will immediately grasp the convenience of not having to obliterate with white out or erase numbers when a change to data is required, either due to error in inputting or observation. We are no longer adding and subtracting exact figures, but now are working with variables by combining the values in a particular cell.

Simply alter the data...and the computing machine utilizes the formula to undertake the calculations so as to immediately yield the required information: because, though the salary might now be $350 instead of $200, it is still "C4" and E3+C4+D4 = Balance E4, regardless of whether C4 is $200 or

$350. And E4+C5+D5 = Balance E5, whether or not E4 is $750 or $600 or anything else.

	A	B	C	D	E
1	DATE	NOTE	INCOME	EXPENSE	BALANCE
2	1/1	Inventory			$500
3	1/1	Grocery		$100	=E2+C3+D3
4	1/2	Salary	$350		=E3+C4+D4
5	1/3	Insurance		$20	=E4+C5+D5

This is particularly important for prognostication: for anticipating the future. If you want to know what your balance will be in 60 days if you bought something unusual, you can input future data based upon your best assumptions on regular income and regular expenses, and then have the computer calculate the future balance for you instantly when you change one of the regular expenses into something unusually large. For example, we now now that if our salary increased $150, our balance on January 2 would be $750. Or, that we can spend up to $580 more at the grocery store without running out of money on January 3.

Adding lines of future or present is also easy: the computer helps you insert them where needed. And, with the sort function you can simply add the data at the bottom, and then highlighting the spreadsheet, sort by date - the computer will place the data in the correct spot, redo the calculations, and produce information required to understand what your balance will be at any given time.

Graphical representations are easily produced using computing machines and spreadsheets, and numerous forms of analysis are possible to accomplish in a fraction of the time it takes to compute by hand.

Sum all the income to see how much your gross income is. If it is a business account, sum your expenses to see what your adjusted business income is. Create a new column and indicate if it is a medical expense which is permitted to be deducted on Schedule A, and you can have the computing machine sort all medical expenses together, so you can easily sum them for your taxes. Sort out all your grocery expenses and see if your bill goes up and down by season, or time of year, and understand how you can rein in your costs.

But this is better discussed in the next section, Reducing Expenses and Waste with Registers.

Chapter 4: Reducing Expenses and Waste with Registers

CHAPTER SUMMARY

Skills of data categorization are introduced, with specific monetary application to tax expenses, and a specific non-monetary application to food waste. Basic analysis techniques are introduced, together with methodology for applying these techniques to reduce expenses. Skills required to prepare two different types of reports, one for their taxes, and one for their household members also involved in decision making processes which impact food waste, are introduced.

Skills of data categorization and application to taxes and food waste

What is a category of data? What is the accuracy of data? Examples of income, expense, dates, non-quantitative data

With the development of computational mathematics, data began to be categorized so as to be better used as variables for calculation in computational equations.

So, if the equation was income - expense = profit, data was organized into categories of incomes, expenses, and profits: the purchase of apples would be an expense, the sale of those apples would be income, and the profits could then be calculated using the computation given.

Therefore, data is organized according to its intended use: the equation describes the categories of data.

If there is data which is not needed for the equation, it is understood as irrelevant.

However, what is irrelevant for one equation is not necessarily entirely irrelevant, and may be useful for a different equation. Therefore, common methodologies include compartmentalization or storage of irrelevant data for when and if it may be needed: the rule which should be followed is that all data should be collected, but not all data should be used.

The methods of collection matter greatly: some data is worth less or even without worth if collected poorly. For example, if you were to only sometimes observe when apples were bought, and not register every expense of apples, then your ability to calculate profit is handicapped.

But, because it is a rare thing for data to be collected perfectly, we tolerate some error, and understand that most calculations will be close approximations to reality, rather than accurate representations. Getting these approximations close enough to reality that they are useful is the goal of data collection.

There is no quantitative standard by which usefulness is considered, though the accuracy of data may be quantified. For some applications, we require almost perfect or perfect accuracy, for others, we may tolerate a 5% or even 20% error rate. For others, we can "be in the ballpark" or "in the neighborhood" (whatever that quantitatively means).

In example, if we were to categorize temporal data, the times at which things occurred, we generally find it sufficient to say that all transactions which occurred between the start of business and the end of business occur on the same "day." But if we are auditing an employee to determine if they have committed an error or even theft, it becomes very important to measure transactions by hour, or even minute - since more than one employee might work a shift that day.

For soft data, or non-quantitative data, our notes and journal entries should be accurate enough to develop quantitative information from: the goal is to bring non-quantitative or soft data into hard numbers.

In example, in our journal, we might remark that food in our refrigerator was bought on tuesday, began to smell bad on thursday, and spoiled so bad by friday it had to be thrown out. If we see this pattern week after week, we can measure this and understand that food was fresh only for 3 days: we have converted the soft data into hard numbers, and this is useful -

because we know to only buy 3 days worth of food at a time if we would avoid throwing food out for spoilage.

Methodology of categorization

The method for registering categories in the ledger is to produce new columns, frequently to the right of the balance - out of the way, compartmentalized and stored, ready for use. If we are categorizing data for the calculation of our tax deduction, for example, we would create columns for medical expenses, mortgage interest payments, business expenses, and the like: the IRS form directs us to develop these categories, or variables, if we would use their method of computation to calculate our deduction.

When using spreadsheets, summing the amount in each column is easy, and advanced analysis, such as correlating one type of expense to another, becomes possible. It might be that we notice that our moving expenses have a high degree of correlation to our expenses of restaurants - we ate out during the moving process because our kitchen supplies were in boxes and we were too tired to remove them to cook... and anticipate these expenses in our next move. Or correlate our utility expenses to some times of year, and plan ahead for higher utility costs in the winter and summer seasons.

This planning ahead is accomplished in the manner described before: inputting future data in advance, we can adjust the anticipated utility expense for summer or winter as being higher, and let the computing machine calculate our new balance at that future data. Will you run out of money? It would be prudent, then, to cut back on some other discretionary costs now, and recalculate until you can avoid the necessity for debt.

The self-control and discipline required to keep to this budget properly belongs elsewhere: many people struggle with financial anxiety, financial irrationality, low impulse control, and other problems which exacerbate their poverty. However, foresight is something which the ledger can assist with.

Reducing expenses using ledgers

Poverty has many causes, and is itself the proximate cause to numerous forms of distress and suffering: poverty exposes a person to crime, illness, premature death, and powerlessness. And poverty can result in a cycle of indebtedness that worsens the poverty, and becomes impossible to escape from. Poverty is dangerous.

It is not always possible to escape poverty.

Sometimes income is insufficient for basic material needs. However, it is possible to ensure that income exceeds expenses - and it is possible to avoid debt, if one is willing to tolerate the pain of poverty and lack of sufficient material needs.

Income - Expenses = Profit. Keeping a household profitable is the primary objective of its financial leadership, the father or mother of the house. Keeping a business profitable is the primary objective of its financial leadership, its Executives.

The undisputed fact of thousands of years of economics is that it is always easier reduce expenses than it is to increase income. This is because income is obtained only by commerce, industry or theft, but there is an almost infinite variety in the ways that expenses may be reduced.

The ledger is a powerful tool in observing opportunities for reducing expenses and avoiding debt, as well as alleviating the suffering of poverty: it is the method by which profit is best calculated, and obtained.

The methodology is systematic.

First, categorize your expenses, and then organize these categories into expenses which are discretionary, and nondiscretionary: those expenses which are choices, and those which are necessary for physical and mental health.

Divide nondiscretionary expenses into those for which alternative suppliers exist, and those which must be obtained from a single source. In this category include those expenses for opulence: Opulences are those expenses which are not entirely optional, and serve social purposes: as a professional might need maintain an expensive set of clothes or vehicles to impress their competence upon clients and coworkers. Or how conspicuous donations to charity, or public service are used to demonstrate character.

The debate as to whether pleasures are luxuries or necessities is as old as time itself, and will not be resolved here. It will be simply addressed as being the philosophical consideration of the financial leadership. However, it may help to understand that luxuries are those expenses which are entirely optional, and which are spent to solely for the purpose of enjoyment - whereas pleasures are those which have a necessary maintenance of mental and physical health. A soap which is softer on the skin is not necessarily a luxury if skin disease results from on using that soap.

The reason why it is important to consider if alternative vendors are available is because of the economic principle of monopoly and discrimination: where there are one or only a few vendors, the buyer is frequently required to pay the most they can afford to. Discovering either alternative products or alternative vendors is important to reducing costs, and is the principle of a type of business science called "purchasing."

Purchasing is a vast science, and cannot be adequately addressed here in any brevity. However, a competent purchaser will not only identify the prices of required items at alternative vendors (compensating for the costs of transportation or shipping), but will undertake a scientific process of engineering to understand the use and purpose of the required item to learn whether it cannot be more cheaply obtained in parts for assembly, or whether a different item would suffice.

The financial manager uses a ledger to identify these items in advance and communicate these needs to the purchaser with enough time to develop alternatives.

The ledger is also used to identify those items which compose a larger part of the entire expenses: savings in these areas of greater expense will have a larger impact on the overall expenses than those expenditures which compose a smaller part of the total expenses.

For example, if expenses on vehicle maintenance amounts to 10% of total expenses, and expenses on groceries amounts to 40% of total expenses, if the purchaser were to find a way to save 25% on one or the other, saving 25% on the vehicle maintenance would reduce the total expenditures by only 2.5%, whereas a 25% savings in groceries would reduce total expenditures by 10%.

In the ledger, simply add the costs of various expenses by column and see where you spend most of your money. Have your household or business purchaser target these larger expenses for reduction first.

The purchaser will also consider the secondary effects of a change in supply. If rent expenses can be reduced by $500 per month by moving further outside the city, but result in $600 more per month in transportation expenses, the loss of $100 would persuade the purchaser to not advise this alternative. Or, if moving to a smaller premises would result in a savings of $200 per month, but also a cost of $300 per month in storage costs, the purchaser would not advise this option, either.

While this seems straight forward, the ledger helps in understanding distant temporal effects: if a vehicle is to be purchased, the purchaser will use the ledger to consider the long-term maintenance even years down the road.

The fundamental principle of purchasing is that vertical integration results in greater efficiencies: by cutting out middlemen and retailers, developing close relationships with suppliers, and even producing those resources required, greater profit is obtained. The financial manager always lets this guide their vertical expansion.

Principles of preparing a report

To be held accountable

It should be evident by now that everyone in the household or business uses the ledger - not just the financial leadership, not just the purchaser. Ledgers facilitate coordination throughout the household or business organization - and help each person be accountable to everyone else. It helps everyone hold everyone else accountable, that they may always do their best. It helps everyone obtain the resources and help they need.

Empower others to understand sufficiently for analysis, decision making and action within their role

The purpose of a ledger is this accountability. But modifying this central and shared document requires a method of communication called the "report." Reports were first developed by the Romans, who used it to describe information which was intended to be "carried back" (the literal definition of "reportare") to the decision makers: because, though the ledger is shared and central to every person in an organization, it is ultimately controlled by the financial leader, and just because one department or person wishes to increase or decrease an expense doesn't mean that they can: a child may want one more toy and suggest that the family buy less vegetables to provide for this expense, however, the financial leader would nix this as fewer vegetables would result in more healthcare expenses and that toy might be a luxury expense.

Consequently, the purpose of reports is prepare the leader for decision making and action within their role: frequently, each department will have their own financial leader responsible for their department's expenditures, or in a house, the head of household will provide a budget to family members responsible for certain household tasks (like grocery shopping, or vehicular maintenance). Therefore, the report should contain sufficient data for analysis, and typically includes an argumentation justifying the recommended expense or change to the future plans in the ledger.

Consider the person's role: to whom and for what are they accountable?

This is why reports will look very different depending on their intended audience: the financial report given by the financial leadership to potential investors will look different than the report given to the purchaser - the purchaser's report to the financial leadership will look different than their report given to the warehouse manager. In a household, the information required by a child is going to be very different than the information required by a partner or spouse.

Even the report you produce for yourself in evaluating a decision will look different based upon what decision you're making: are you buying a house, or a cabbage?

In preparing the report, consider to whom and what are they accountable. What data do they require to make their analysis? What analysis do they require to make their decision?

Sometimes, too, a company or family will have a preferred format for a report, or a preferred style of communication. Some will prefer oral reports, or graphical representations, or particular stylistic considerations.

In general, this may be a good format for organizing your report:

1. OPPORTUNITY. Briefly describe the situation, why is a proposal needed? What is the problem or opportunity?
2. CONCLUSION OF PROPOSAL / SOLUTION. Briefly describe what you are suggesting be done: this is your conclusion. What do you think needs to be done differently, what do you think needs to be bought, etc.?

3. MOTIVATION. Briefly summarize your analysis: what are the costs and benefits of this proposal?
4. RISKS. Assess the feasibility of your proposal: what are the risks if this is implemented, and if not implemented? Will this work as planned?
5. DATA. Provide data required for analysis and evaluate the accuracy of the data presented.
6. RESEARCH. Provide your method of investigation and research: how did you obtain your data?
7. ANALYSIS. Show your method of analysis: how did you reach your conclusion?
8. EVIDENCE. Provide evidence from tests or comparisons from others who have attempted something similar which either support or contradict the conclusions.
9. CONTACT INFORMATION. Who worked on the report, who can be contacted for more information?

Don't be overwhelmed by the extensive nature of this outline: most reports will be simple.

For example, a simple oral presentation might be as simple as saying at a board meeting or household meeting, "I think our coffee is too expensive. I checked, and if we buy the same coffee wholesale, we can save 20%. If we switch brands, we can save 40%. Here's the price sheets I obtained, they are current as of yesterday. I brewed a test pot of the new coffee yesterday, and no one even noticed - and here's some other reviews on the new brand of coffee saying it tastes just as good." Such a presentation is very convincing: the financial leader would likely approve.

Color coding

A useful method of easing visual inspection of the ledger on a spreadsheet is to use color coding to indicate the department or person who should be paying special attention to that information, or to separate out hypothetical changes to the ledger in preparing experimental scenarios of "before and after" for presentations. Being able to see, at a glance, the different kinds of expenses helps associate them with each other and reveal patterns which otherwise might have been missed.

Chapter 5: Improving Efficiency with Registers

CHAPTER SUMMARY

Previous examples are used to learn skills of calculation required to improve efficiencies in expenses and to distinguish surplus resources from delayed costs. Basic financial strategies for how to acquire these surplus resources for use and how to reduce inefficiency are introduced, including the "savings account" for emergency expenses and bulk purchasing.

Management theory

A manager is a person who is responsible to the company or household to ensure efficiency by supporting the transport of resources to where they are required in the company or household and transporting waste from the places of origin. To some extent, the financial leader is naturally a manager of the entire company, but this is really a specialized position - in the same way that a purchaser is a specialized position, but the financial manager has as a part of their responsibilities purchasing.

The science of management is complex, requiring a comprehensive understanding of statistical mathematics, but the principles are easy enough to convey succinctly.

Efficiency is the measurement of how many resources are required to develop or produce another resource: as the quantity of resources required for conversion diminishes, efficiency increases. The surplus resources required for conversion are understood as "waste."

If you require a pound of apple for a pie, and have to get 1.5 pounds of large apples and 2 pounds of small apples (because of the larger core to volume ratio of the small apples), it is possible to understand the larger apples are 25% more efficient: 1.5 lbs large apples / 2 lbs small apples = ¾: ¼ lbs fewer pounds are required. If the price of the larger apples is less than 25% more expensive than small apples, a savings would be observed.

Examining the efficiency of one system over another through time, we start to observe that the system which requires the fewest resources will be the most efficient. In other words, laziness - so long as productivity is not diminished more than the cost of busy productivity - is profitable. The efficiency of efficiency is the objective of efficiency analysis: the financial leader should not be more efficient if it costs more to be.

Quality should also be considered. If smaller apples are cheaper but produce a lower quality pie, and those lower quality pies do not sell as well as pies made with large apples, it will be more expensive in the long term to produce cheaper pies.

Another principle to consider besides reduction is that recycling is profitable. If waste can be recaptured and repurposed, it is no longer waste. If the cores of those apples, for example, can be used to produce vinegar or apple butter, the money used to buy the whole apple is now not being wasted at all: the money bought not only the meat of the apple, but its core too.

This is why it is always in the interests of businesses to let the need for recycling, repurposing and recapturing in management guide its horizontal expansion - in the same way that profitability in purchasing guides vertical expansion.

Here we begin to see the vital role of the manager and purchaser in a company: for without expansion, vertical and horizontal, profit stagnates. And it is the fundamental responsibility of the financial leader to always expand profit.

Method of analysis: the regression

Analysis of regressive equation: understanding relative importance

As the ledger was used previously to identify large expenses for targeting for reduced costs through purchasing, the ledger is also used to understand the relative importance of resources. Which is more important to a household: broccoli or milk? Milk or rent? Which is more important to a pie company: apples or sugar? Or skilled cooks?

In determining the importance of costs, the purchaser utilized correlation to anticipate cash flow. Here, the manager will use regressive analysis to define the quantitative value of every resource.

Though this is advanced mathematics, as with correlation, we may simply the process to understanding trends.

In example, let's use a pie that sells for $10. If a pie's cost is understood as the result of combining **A**pples, **S**ugar, **F**lour, **O**il, oven **H**eat and **P**ackaging, we understand the calculation as being:

$$A + S + F + O + H + P = \text{Pie Cost}$$

We then place a cost to each of these...

$$\$2 + \$0.50 + \$0.25 + \$0.15 + \$1 + \$0.75 = \$4.65$$

So, if it sells for $10, where does this extra $5.35 come from? We have obviously missed a few variables. Labor might come to mind, but if that labor only costs a dollar or two, we still come up short. We eventually determine that we have identified all the missing variables - and conclude that it is the combination of these which affects value. A cook is only good as their ingredients, and the ingredients are worthless in the hands of a bad cook. Marketing plays a role. Etc.

Experimentation here is of importance: data is required to study the matter. Altering one or more of these variables in quality quickly reveals changes to the price the pie will fetch. Perhaps we substitute the green apples for red apples and notice that we sell fewer pies, having to reduce the price a dollar? Then we know that red apples are worth a $1 in profit. If we were to substitute cooks, and the inexperienced cook loses $5 dollars per pie, we know that the cook is worth $5 in profit. We can then compare cooks to apples: we can say with certainty that the cook is worth more than apples. And we can even speculate that the cook is worth to the profitability of each pie perhaps five times more than the apples.

We can also objectively compare employees and undertake management of them better. If we notice that one employee underperforms with statistical significance, we can focus our effort in understanding why. It may be that one cook lacks eye glasses to see the measurements on a measuring cup, and providing eye glasses would bring that employee up to average or above average performance. It might be that that employee's knife is needing sharpened, slowing them down - sharpening the knife would improve efficiency.

Capitalism

Sometimes spending money results in more profitability. When we purchase things which result in profit, this is a purchase of capital.

Capital = assets - liabilities. So how does incurring a liability result in more capital? Capital purchases represent "negative" liabilities: the value of profit each of these purchases gains is an asset. This is why the philosophy of capitalism directs its adherents to pursue profits: by improving profitability, capital is increased.

And, long term investments to profitability do frequently pay more than short-sighted cutbacks: it does not matter if the company or family earns $10 this year if they cannot do that every year. The family or company that earns $1 every year will earn more in 11 years than the company or family that earns $10 one year and nothing for 9 years following. The shortsighted company or family will be bankrupted, and broken.

Dependent Variable

In regression analysis, we must identify the dependent variable: the experimental variable. What is changing, and how does it affect the other variables to result in more or less profit?

Independent Variable

Independent variables are those variables held constant during the experiment. These are held constant so that changes to the single dependent variable can be accurately compared against each other. If we used large apples and brown sugar in one experiment and small apples and white sugar in the other, how would we know whether it was the apples or the sugar which resulted in greater profit?

The most important independent variable is time: it permits us to observe changes as they take affect, and identify possible interactions with other independent variables.

In any experiment, try to hold all things constant except the dependent or experimental variable.

It is also advisable to control for mistakes in implementation by both repeating the experiment (sometimes not all other variables are controlled - perhaps one year the apples taste better than other years, for example), and to divide the experiment into two groups: one in which the change is experimented with, and one in which the change is not experimented with. This will allow you to presume that both the "control" group and experimental group are affected by the same independent variables.

Analysis

Because the ratio of the dependent to independent variable is always accomplished by division, it allows direct comparison of unlike outcomes (pies): the brown sugar pie and the white sugar pie can be directly compared, if the white sugar experiment increases profit 25% above brown sugar pies. Similarly, we can observe the average efficiency of many different employees to see the standard deviation and reveal outliers.

What is setting the best employees apart from the underperformers? It is not enough to simply reward excellence. It must be reproduced. It is not enough to cull low performers, if the cause for underperformance is not understood, the next employee may also underperform with the same dull knife. It is not enough to say white sugar pies are more profitable: understanding the reason why will help you make better pies.

This analysis requires additional research and experimentation: switch out the knife, observe.

But the data always comes from the ledger, which tracks every employee's productivity, every pie's value, every ingredient in distinct columns.

Analysis of regressive equation: understanding trends

When data is organized by date, we may sometimes see trends: perhaps profits are decreasing gradually through the winter as the supply of fresh apples is difficult to secure? Perhaps it is always increasing, and in correlation to marketing efforts? The manager can then understand the efficiency or limitations of marketing, or the need to secure a better supply of apples. Understanding these trends is the role of the manager, who must analyze them in the context of waste and resources.

Surplus resources

Calculating if a resource is surplus

Besides waste, the manager may need to contend with surplus resources.

A surplus resource is a resource whose storage costs equals or exceeds its utility or value. It is not worth keeping.

Though it may be "wasteful," the intelligent manager will get rid of these surplus resources before the costs of storage accumulate further - and while throwing them out might make sense, the wiser manager will sell these resources for some minimal or token amount rather than give them away totally to waste.

Managing resources means ensuring surplus resources are not acquired in the first place.

This said, sometimes there is no cost to storage and it makes sense to lock in a large supply of resources in the warehouse or cupboard or pantry to ensure no interruption: no one wants to run out of diapers, so some extra are always bought and stored. They don't go bad. And cost nothing to keep.

Introduction to finance

A manager has to make sure that resources are available not only where required, but when.

This is the principle of finance: to ensure that resources are available when they are required. A financial manager is responsible for ensuring that future cash flows are brought to the present when they are needed.

The cost of bringing future cash flows to the present can be expensive: this is accomplished by borrowing through debt, selling an interest in revenues or assets through stock, or even mortgaging real property.

A typically family does not have the hundreds of thousands of dollars required to buy a house - but they will borrow from the future to the present need by way of a debt and mortgage. A company might need start up capital: they will have money in the future from selling pies, so they borrow from the future to the present by way of a start up loan. In the future, the debts are repaid.

The financier, the person whose occupation is to facilitate this transfer, frequently charges an interest rate above the expected inflation rate. When the costs of borrowing exceed the anticipated future cash value, the financial manager should decline the loan.

Loaning resources and money is profitable, and the wise financial manager will advise the financial leader of their home or business to undertake financing when possible: purchasing stocks, shares in mutual funds, loaning money to family or trusted friends, etc. is a good use of money and resources when there is more available than is needed in the present time.

An alternative is the savings account: surplus money can be put into a savings account, and effectively warehoused until required.

Insurance is also a good investment for this reason: by providing less than the actual cost of an emergency expense to an insurer, the insurer accepts the risk that the emergency will take place, and the insured benefits in the future with present dollars: the cost of risk is cheaper in the past than in the moment of crisis.

Having resources when they are required: preventing interruption

The financial manager ensures that not only future money, but future resources are made available as necessary. This is done through warehousing: surplus resources are intentionally purchased and stored at expense to ensure that they are available at a point in time. An interruption in supply can be costly: and if this cost of interruption is greater than the costs of storage, the manager will warehouse surplus resources to prevent interruption.

In a household this is frequently done with milk, bread and other staples: during bad weather, supply may be interrupted, and staple foods are stockpiled, even at risk of spoilage, even at costs of refrigeration, to prevent that interruption.

In most businesses that rent premises, the landlord will require the manager stockpile the facility, by contracting for or even paying rent a year at a time. It is expensive for a landlord to have an interruption in tenancy.

The savings account is effectively the warehousing of money: putting money aside for emergencies prevents an interruption of money supplies, and the cost of borrowing money in an emergency.

Anticipating future expenses by putting them aside into a savings account has the same effect: if you know that electrical costs are going to be higher in the summer, putting aside extra money in the spring prevents an interruption. Or, if a new vehicle will eventually need 100,000 mile maintenance, putting aside a little toward that every month brings past money to the future when it will be needed for that unusual expense.

Bulk purchases are also similar: buying a vast quantity of beans results in cheaper beans per pound, and warehousing them allows those beans to be accessed when needed: the savings per pound will hopefully exceed the costs of storage, but you are effectively buying tomorrow's dinner with today's dollars because it is cheaper today than tomorrow.

Using ledger for financial analysis

Inputting the costs of borrowing or the income from lending into the ledger is easy, using the same method as has already been introduced. It permits the analysis of whether the balance permits this activity.

Chapter 6: Resource Theory

CHAPTER SUMMARY

Skills of economics are introduced to understand why it is easier to reduce waste and expense of existing money and resources than to acquire new money and resources, and to recognize renewable and non-renewable resources used in home and business through ledgers.

Introduction to economics

Economics is not only the science of resource production, transfer and consumption, but is the means of measuring prosperity.

Here it is important to distinguish between prosperity and profitability: prosperity is the enjoyment of that profit. As introduced at the beginning, prosperity is the purpose for which profit is sought.

We have observed through understanding efficient efficiency that a penny saved is a penny earned, and it is not worth a dollar to save a penny. We have understood the importance of having money when it is required. Management and leadership have been thoroughly introduced. The shareholder, the financier, has also been introduced. In doing so we have examined the role of the ledger in the production of resources, whether by commerce and trade or industry through purchasing, and the transfer of resources through management.

What remains is the stakeholder: the consumer. In a family, this is best represented by the household: children are pure consumers, contributing little to the household's resources. To some extent, the adults in a household are both consumers and producers of resources. In a business, the clients and customers are, of course, consumers, but so are the employees and even those people of the city who are impacted by the business.

These consumers are guided by a principle of emergy.

Emergy is the amount of energy that was consumed in direct and indirect transformations to make a product or service. Emergy is a measure of quality differences between different forms of energy.

The theory of Emergy is that the difficulty of acquiring something is its true value: an apple may cost a dollar, but if it is a hassle to go to the store, and you have only one apple left, you might save that apple to eat as if it were worth more than a dollar - because it represents the greater cost of obtaining more apples.

The idea that non-renewable resources have more costs associated with them than renewable resources explains why the last minutes of a game in gambling are more valuable than the first minutes, associated with greater costs of risks: with fewer minutes, there are fewer opportunities to recover losses, and so smart gamblers will become more conservative toward the end of a game and more risk-taking in the beginning.

In investing, too, a person should take more risks with their portfolio at the beginning of their career than toward the end: there are fewer years to recover losses, and also because investing is essentially financing, loaning current dollars to the future, there is less future to loan toward.

Emergy encourages the question of whether it is worth spending money to save money? What is the worth of a dollar? Do you want an apple? Or are you content?

Emergy explains contentment, prosperity, does not motivate the acquisition of another apple, another dollar.

It is similar to the ancient Buddhist wisdom: contentment is indeed the greatest wealth, for someone who is content is less impoverished than someone who has more money and is discontent. The Buddhists teach that generosity is the means to contentment, and frugality the means to generosity. Both are founded in a practice of kindness, and compassion.

On a practical level, beyond philosophy, as a person develops their generosity, they understand they can make due with less, and become more efficient, and conquer their financial anxiety. They develop self-control through frugality: guided by kindness, they understand how to provide for their needs, physical and mental. They understand the difference between comfort or pleasure and luxury.

The questions of emergy ultimately become guided to answers by a philosophy of utilitarianism. What use is the money, the resources, the apples, the pies? What is the object of acquisition, of profit? If resources are simply going to be depleted, why acquire them in the first place?

Some argue that a life lived in contentment, unproductive, is wasted potential. But remembering that so long as the cost of waste is less than the cost of income, it is observed that for the content person, the disruption to their prosperity and happiness by being more productive makes productivity irrational.

Recognizing renewable and non-renewable resources

Theory of exhaustion

Emergy divides resources into renewable and non-renewable resources.

Non-renewable resources can theoretically be exhausted through use (are limited in supply or availability) or possess costs to renewing their supply. There is value in conserving non-renewable resources, whereas there is no incentive to conserve non-renewable resources.

Here it is important to note that all resources are theoretically non-renewable, as they have lifetimes in which they will wear out and break beyond repair, requiring replacement. Even the sun will go dark one day.

Which is why the term must be considered with emergetics: the duration of a budget cycle of a salary period will reveal different non-renewable resources than a period of 10 years, or even an intergenerational span of several hundred years (as is common on some lumber farms and mines, or in several multinational companies). Will a resource be exhausted in that time period is the question considered.

For example, it is unlikely that a car will be exhausted during your next pay period. But it is likely that the car will be exhausted sometime in the next 25 years. During the next two weeks, it is a renewable resource; during the next 25 years, it is non-renewable. Daylight will run out today, but will renew tomorrow. Are we planning for today, or for the next week?

Households frequently find their pantries run out before their salary is paid; preventing this requires treating food as a non-renewable resource and looking at planning beyond the pay period to ensure adequate supplies are acquired for the next pay period.

Electricity is non-renewable, every kilowatt used is gone forever, and costs money to replace. So it is smart to conserve these kilowatts: the incentive to conserve electricity is very strong because the period is instantaneous.

A giant 50lb bag of rice.is essentially a renewable resource for a small family, providing food for a very long time - but the last box of spaghetti comes with a strong incentive to conserve because when it is gone, it must be replaced immediately..

To some extent these costs of replacement incentivizing conservation are psychological, but there is real monetary value: money saved is money earned, and the inclination to increase profit discourages expense - and especially the procrastination of expenses. Money spent cannot be spent on anything else, or earn interest. This loss of opportunity and earning is a real penalty.

Calculating point of exhaustion: the intersection with zero

The point of exhaustion may be calculated using a ledger by tracking the inventory of the item. Instead of registering dollar expenses, a 50lb bag of rice might be tracked using pounds or ounces: as the bag is consumed, the register subtracts from the 50lbs what is taken from it.

Examining this data against the dates these entries occur, one can develop a linear understanding of its trend: $ax+b = c$ is the standard form of a linear equation. Here, the average rate at which the rice is used or depleted is a, the dates are x, and the constant b is the initial inventory: c is the point on the line to be calculated. If the rice is depleted at a rate of 2 pounds every week, we see... $-2x+50 = c$. If we wanted to know how many weeks it would take for c to equal zero - how long to deplete the entire bag, we calculate 50 / 2 = 25 weeks. And plan in our ledger to buy a new 50 pound bag just before then.

We can calculate the exhaustion of money in the same way, when our expenses exceed our income: examine the register for the data you require to develop the average rate of depletion.

Or we can calculate when our assets will grow enough to retire, if our income exceeds our expenses: look to the register and develop the average rate of accumulation.

Sometimes the rate of change is not linear, but is expressed through more complex algebra. While this is not an instructional book on how to develop an accurate regression of the data, it is worth noting that many spreadsheet programs have functionality included to assist in this regressive analysis.

Regressive analysis on increasing inefficiency

If we were to increase our efficiency, we would notice that resources are depleted at a decreasing rate, or that there is a difference in the rate at which they are exhausted. Comparing before and after, we may report that our changes should be retained, or not - or even understand why they failed or succeeded.

The emergency expense (unanticipated zeroing of resource)

Sometimes resources unexpectedly exhaust: if a major health incident occurred without insurance, a family's assets could be exhausted in an instant. Or if one income earner in the family were to die, the expenses could quickly overtake the income and deplete the assets.

These are emergency expenses, and while many emergencies are of the small kind (someone forgot a lunch and needs to make an unanticipated restaurant purchase), it is possible to see whether these expenses generally conform to expectations and know for certain whether they were truly emergencies.

Sometimes, a person always forgets their lunch - and are not honest enough with themselves to admit this is the normal, rather than the exceptional emergency. The regression won't lie: it will show that these restaurant purchases could be anticipated as normal trends.

Theory: reduce use of non-renewable resources, rely on renewable resources

The theory of emergetics teaches to reduce reliance on non-renewable resources - not only because they are more costly, but because they may suddenly deplete in an emergency and are therefore infinitely less reliable than renewable resources which cannot deplete at all.

Conclusion: Capitalism

This concludes an introduction to the ledger, and a basic introduction to business principles and philosophy. What remains is only a brief remark upon the value of ethicality: for without ethics, philosophy and science is worthless. The system by which we shall judge the morality of business is "capitalism."

Capitalism is, as the name suggests, a method of business by which profit is expended into capital: non-profits represent the urgently necessary development of business to the understanding that competition eventually brings profit levels to a minimum, and it is also by competition that resources become scarce enough to drive up costs of business.

Therefore, it is by service alone that a business prospers.

While non-profit business is a subject which I fully develop in subsequent book, it may be enough here for you to understand that it was not only to inspire you to take ownership of the numerous problems of our society, but to show you the skills needed to succeed in this, that this book was written. For your sake, and all our sakes, I wish you success and prosperity!

There is both value and necessity in love, kindness and generosity. This real value to friendship discourages a destructive form of competition. The success and prosperity of any one can become the foundation of the success and prosperity of an entire civilization.

As you will discover, the ability of any person to control their world is severely limited. Therefore, it is in their selfish interests to improve their world and make it an environment which, if not conducive to their life and business, is at least not hostile.

Domination and force are expensive, and peace purchased by these is non-renewable. Therefore, rather than conquest and occupation, whether through monopolization or private-public partnerships in facism, the intelligent business will look toward collaboration, cooperation, and non profit business models to answer their needs.

See: as vertical and horizontal expansion are guided by the acts of management and purchasing, conflict and competition guide the business toward diversification into non profit enterprise. The necessary consequence of capitalist theory is the private ownership of not only all property, but the problems of society as well.

In this non-profit model of business, profit is sought to be minimized: the principles are the same, though, so since expenses are more easily controlled than income (which may come from enterprise or donations), expenses are raised or avenues of income are sacrificed for the primary objective (which is not profit). For example, an artist will sacrifice income by taking low paying jobs to support their artistic endeavors, or a religious organization might expend all their funds to provide food and other support for the poor. A trust might maintain its balance of assets and purposefully distribute its excess income.

Therefore, I would conclude this instruction on the ledger best by encouraging you to implement what you have learned, and undertaking capitalism yourself, discover the boundless prosperity of our magnificent age: for in doing so I have no doubt but that you will, as I have, understand the value in Love: whoever loves Love truly truly can do no wrong, for all will be forgiven of them, and whatever you risk in Love's worthwhile service by non-profit enterprise will be justified by the urgent necessity of the work. Be confident and bold.

Aaron Scott Brachfeld Michelson
Grand Junction, Colorado 2019

www.ingramcontent.com/pod-product-compliance
Lightning Source LLC
Chambersburg PA
CBHW030954240526
45463CB00016B/2553